THE HEROES AND MORTALS OF GREEK MYTHOLOGY

by Don Nardo

COMPASS POINT BOOKS

a capstone imprint

Compass Point Books
151 Good Counsel Drive
P.O. Box 669
Mankato, MN 56002-0669

Editors: Sarah Eason and Geoff Barker
Designers: Paul Myerscough and Simon Borrough
Media Researcher: Susannah Jayes
Content Consultant: Michael Vickers, DLitt, Professor of Archaeology, University of Oxford
Production Specialist: Laura Manthe

Image Credits
Alamy: Blickwinkel 46–47, Interfoto 34, Ivy Close Images 22, 44–45, North Wind Picture Archives 4;
Bridgeman: Alte Pinakothek, Munich, Germany 55, Private Collection 41, 56–57, Walters Art
Museum 37; **Corbis:** The Art Archive 23, Bettmann 38, Stefano Bianchetti 10, Heritage Images 39;
Geoff Ward: cover (front), 7, 12–13, 20–21, 25, 35, 51; **Getty:** The Bridgeman Art Library 31, 32;
Istock: Paolo Gaetano 28–29, GaryWG chapter 2 bgd, 62–63; **NASA:** Goddard Space Flight Center
Scientific Visualization Studio 48–49 (Jupiter & moons); **Shutterstock:** Clearviewstock 48–49,
Eugeneharnam 26–27, Ralf Hirsch 17, Jbor 52, Georgios Kollidas 42 (front), Vladimir Korostyshevskiy
1, 9, pASob 58–59, Pavelk 42–43, Jozef Sedmak 19 (front), Simfalex cover (back), Brigida Soriano 15,
Stonyanh chapter 1 bgd, 60–61, Elena Yakusheva 18–19.

Library of Congress Cataloging-in-Publication Data
Nardo, Don, 1947–
  The heroes and mortals of Greek mythology / by Don Nardo.
     p. cm. —(Ancient Greek mythology)
  Includes bibliographical references and index.
  ISBN 978-0-7565-4480-5 (library binding)
  1. Heroes—Juvenile literature. 2. Greek mythology—Juvenile literature. I. Title. II. Series.
  BL795.H46N37 2012
  398.220938—dc22   2011015245

Visit Compass Point Books on the Internet at *www.capstonepub.com*

Printed in the United States of America in Stevens Point, Wisconsin.
032011
006111WZF11

TABLE OF CONTENTS

Chapter 1
TRULY TIMELESS TALES

Throughout human history, each of the world's many lands and peoples has developed its own, individual folklore or mythology. These mythologies have often differed from one another in various ways. But they have also displayed some basic similarities. For example, all have featured gods and other divine or supernatural beings. Also typical have been stories about monsters and creatures half-human and half-animal.

Still another element that all mythologies have in common is mortals who interact with the gods and other nonhumans. Most of these mortals are depicted as ordinary, like people in all ages, including the modern one. A few, however, were heroes. A larger-than-life human figure, most often male, a hero was able to accomplish incredibly difficult feats that ordinary people dared not attempt. Often these included hunting down and slaying hideous, terrifying monsters. Mythological heroes also challenged cruel tyrants and removed them from power, bringing freedom to long-oppressed peoples.

The actual deeds achieved by such heroes vary from tale to tale and from one culture to another. Yet all of these champions share certain traits, principles, and goals. First, each possesses integrity in the highest degree. The hero would sooner die than commit dishonorable acts. The universal hero also displays uncommon courage and physical strength. In addition, he frequently performs feats that usually only the gods can accomplish. As a result, the gods take notice and often get involved in the action. Sometimes they help the hero; other times they try to keep him from accomplishing his goal.

Ancient Greeks, including Homer, who told the story of Troy, sang tales and poems. They often played a lyre or other musical instrument.

Setting a Good Example

Just as the gods had supposedly done with the heroes and other mortals, the Greeks of classical times attempted to interact with the gods. They did this most often through the rituals of prayer and sacrifice. For them sacrifice consisted of making offerings, such as food, drink, or valuables, to the gods. So when they heard the age-old tales of humans who had attained contact with the divine, they saw those people, especially the heroes, as role models. In a way, an ancient hero set an example for ordinary people. His strength and determination often gave average individuals the courage to try to go beyond their commonplace existence and strive for something better. According to Michael Grant, an expert on ancient cultures, the Greeks

> saw something splendid and superhuman about what they supposed to be their lost past. This seemed to them filled with superb figures living for renown and pursuing it with competitive vigor. [The myths about these heroes showed] that [people] can do amazing things by [their] own effort and by [their] own nature, indeed, that [they] can almost rise above [their] own nature into strengths scarcely known or understood.

Passing on the Past

Throughout the remainder of ancient times, the Greek myths featuring heroes and other mortals were retold in homes and other informal settings and taught in

The Age of Heroes

For the Greeks who lived between about 800 BC and 300 BC, the relationship between the gods and humans was fascinating and thrilling. Most Greeks of that time were very religious. They believed that the gods they worshipped had lived among heroes and other mortals during a period of the distant past. They called it the Age of Heroes. Today historians call it Greece's Bronze Age. They think that some of the characters of Greek mythology might have been based on real kings and other people from that age.

schools. Centuries later, medieval Europeans adopted and repeated them as well. In this way these truly timeless tales eventually passed into the lore and literature of modern peoples, including the French, British, and Americans.

When people today read these tales, they often feel themselves drawn away into more exotic and exciting times and places. As Grant points out, readers can "feel larger than life, freed from the [pressures] of present realities." Mythological characters like the mighty Heracles, greedy Midas, and wily Odysseus, "carry us with them in their struggles and sufferings." Likewise when they triumph over evil and injustice, "so do we."

Monsters are common in Greek mythology. The Gorgons were dreadful creatures, and the most famous Gorgon, Medusa , was slain by the hero Perseus.

7

Chapter 2
THREE FAMOUS HEROES

Of the many heroes populating Greek mythology, Heracles, Theseus, and Jason are perhaps the best known. Heracles (whom the Romans later called Hercules) was unarguably the most accomplished and renowned. According to legend, he was a big bear of a man. Ancient writers variously described him as having a hairy, barrellike chest, a thick beard and mustache, lots of bulging muscles, and enormous physical strength. Part of his huge stature and strength came from his unusual birthright. His mother, Alcmena, was a mortal woman. But his father was Zeus, leader of the Greek Olympian gods. And some of Heracles' great physical prowess was undoubtedly inherited from his divine forebear.

Heracles was adept in the use of many weapons, but his favorite was the bow. He also enjoyed swinging a large, heavy club, which became one of his two main symbols. The other was the magnificent lion skin he often wore.

In addition to his significant physical attributes, Heracles had much strength of character. He was honest, brave, humble, and willing to admit when he was wrong. However, he did possess two character flaws that sometimes got him into trouble. First, he lacked the mental quickness of most other Greek heroes. For example, his friend, the Athenian warrior-king Theseus, was considerably brighter and cleverer. Heracles' other character flaw was his nasty temper. Now and then he lapsed into fits of anger so terrible that anyone who got in his way, even a friend or loved one, was not safe.

In works of art, Heracles is depicted with an incredibly powerful physique.

A Superhuman Child

Heracles was born in the famous Greek city of Thebes, several miles north of Athens. The wily Zeus had earlier impersonated Alcmena's mortal husband, Amphitryon, and gotten her pregnant. Not surprisingly, when Zeus' wife, the goddess Hera, heard that Alcmena bore Zeus' child, she became extremely jealous. Hera ordered the goddess of childbirth, Eileithyia, to stop the baby's birth. But that murderous mission failed.

Next Hera sent two monstrous snakes to kill and eat the infant Heracles. That scheme was equally unsuccessful, however. Even as a baby, he was so strong he was able to grab the serpents, one in each hand, and choke the life out of them.

Heracles displayed his supernatural strength when he killed a lion with his bare hands.

Son of Zeus

Witnessing this fantastic feat, Amphitryon concluded that Heracles was no ordinary child. The man consulted a blind prophet named Teiresias, who was known for his wisdom. Teiresias said that the baby was not Amphitryon's but rather the son of the powerful god Zeus.

Feeling that he had been blessed by the gods, Amphitryon lavished attention on Heracles. The boy received an excellent education, and as he grew, experts taught him how to use weapons, including the spear, sword, and bow. They also turned him into a first-rate wrestler. He always won his matches because of his superhuman strength.

That power was further tested when Heracles was in his mid-teens. A large lion began devouring Amphitryon's sheep. So the fearless young man hunted the beast down, seized it, and broke its neck, all with practically no injuries to himself. Then he skinned the fallen creature. From that day on, he wore its handsome hide over his tunic.

The Strongman Marries

As a young man, Heracles continued to accomplish amazing feats of strength and courage. These made him renowned across all of Greece. The king of Thebes, Creon, was so thrilled that he arranged for his daughter, Megara, to marry the strongman. It did not take long for Heracles and his bride to fall madly in love, and in the years that followed they had eight children.

Meanwhile, the queen of the gods, Hera, had not let go of her jealousy and hatred for Heracles. Hoping to rob him of his happy life, she caused him to go temporarily insane. Not realizing what he was doing, he proceeded to kill his beloved wife, Megara, and six of their children.

Crazy with Guilt

As soon as Heracles regained his wits, he saw what he had done and was paralyzed with horror and guilt. He decided that the best way to punish himself for the murders was to take his own life. But just as he was about to do so, his friend Theseus stopped him. Theseus argued that the killings were not murders. After all, he said, Heracles had committed these awful deeds while under Hera's evil influence. Theseus took his comrade to Athens, where the citizens consoled and happily welcomed the famous strongman.

As time went by, however, Heracles could not rid himself of the guilt he felt for slaying his family. So he traveled to Delphi. There, in a temple of the god Apollo, was an oracle, a young woman said to be able to relay messages from the gods. The oracle advised Heracles to journey southward to the region of Argolis. A ruler there, Eurystheus, would assign the strongman 12 seemingly impossible tasks. Only if these were accomplished would Heracles' guilt disappear.

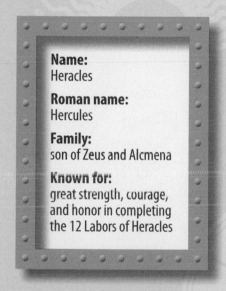

Name:
Heracles

Roman name:
Hercules

Family:
son of Zeus and Alcmena

Known for:
great strength, courage, and honor in completing the 12 Labors of Heracles

The 12 Labors

The man in the lion skin eagerly threw himself into the so-called 12 Labors. The first consisted of killing a gigantic cat, the Nemean Lion. Because it could not be slain by ordinary weapons, he wrestled it to the ground and strangled it. For his second labor, Heracles slew the Hydra, a frightening creature with nine heads. Next he captured and brought back to Eurystheus the Cerynitian Hind, a large male deer, which had horns made of gold.

The nine remaining labors tested all of Heracles' strength, bravery, and resolve. They consisted of capturing a huge, ferocious boar; cleaning the unbelievably filthy and smelly cattle stables of Augeas, king of the Greek city of Elis; chasing away a flock of colossal birds that had been killing livestock and people; and capturing a rampaging bull on the large Greek island of Crete. He also had to tame a herd of man-eating horses; bring back the girdle (belt) of Hippolyta, queen of the Amazons, a famous group of skilled female warriors; and collect the cattle belonging to a three-headed monster named Geryon.

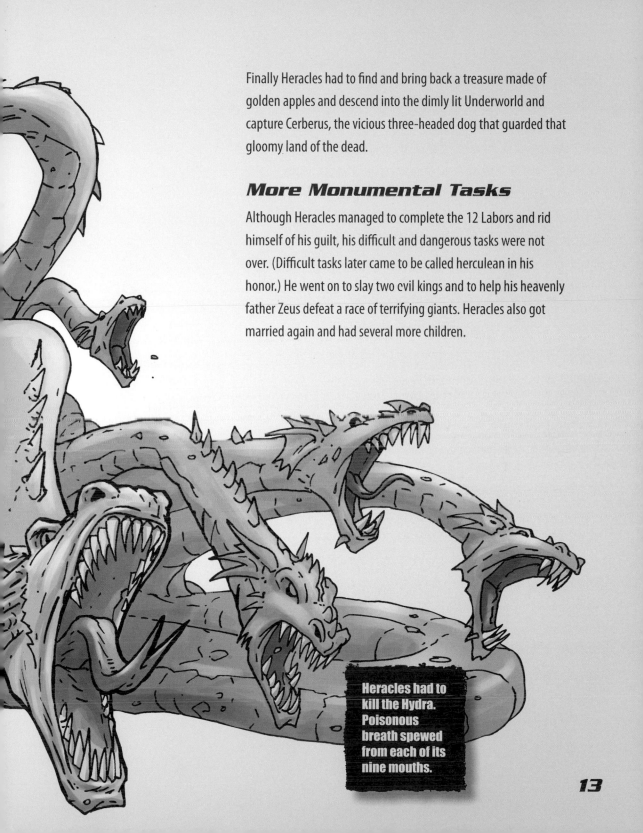

Finally Heracles had to find and bring back a treasure made of golden apples and descend into the dimly lit Underworld and capture Cerberus, the vicious three-headed dog that guarded that gloomy land of the dead.

More Monumental Tasks

Although Heracles managed to complete the 12 Labors and rid himself of his guilt, his difficult and dangerous tasks were not over. (Difficult tasks later came to be called herculean in his honor.) He went on to slay two evil kings and to help his heavenly father Zeus defeat a race of terrifying giants. Heracles also got married again and had several more children.

Heracles had to kill the Hydra. Poisonous breath spewed from each of its nine mouths.

Into the Sky

Unfortunately for the valiant strongman, however, his new wife, Deianira, grew worried that he had fallen in love with another woman. It was not true. But Deianira eventually became convinced of it. As jealous as Hera had once been, she smeared some highly toxic liquid on a tunic. Then the unsuspecting Heracles put on the tunic, which burned him so badly it was clear he would not survive. His children and friends were devastated. But they were soon amazed and relieved when the mighty Zeus gently carried his heroic son into the sky in a column of smoke. Thereafter, the legends say, the big-hearted Heracles enjoyed eternal life.

Theseus the Warrior-king

Heracles' longtime friend, Theseus, was not as big and physically powerful as the famous strongman. But Theseus was no less gallant and daring. He also possessed several other impressive qualities that combined to make him one of the more memorable characters in Greece's Age of Heroes.

First, Theseus was strikingly handsome, which made him particularly attractive to women. He was also highly intelligent and cunning, as well as a courageous warrior and effective king. He proved his abilities as a fighter when he killed one of the scariest monsters ever to terrorize the Greeks. And he showed his talent and wisdom as a ruler after becoming king of Greece's greatest city—Athens.

The King and the Maiden

In fact, in later ages Theseus was long remembered as Athens' state hero. The story of how he earned that status began not long before he was born in Troezen, a town lying several miles south of Athens.

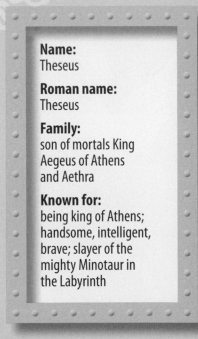

Name:
Theseus

Roman name:
Theseus

Family:
son of mortals King Aegeus of Athens and Aethra

Known for:
being king of Athens; handsome, intelligent, brave; slayer of the mighty Minotaur in the Labyrinth

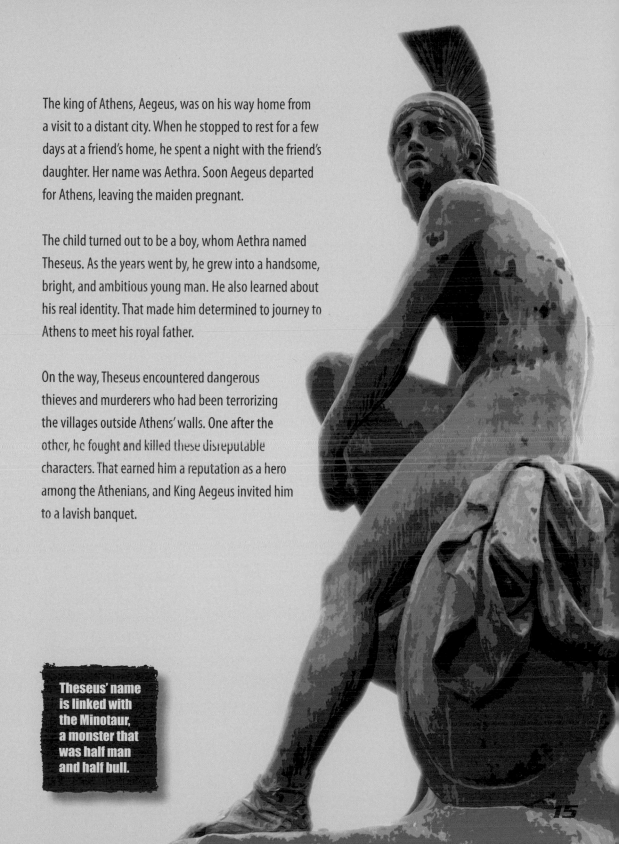

The king of Athens, Aegeus, was on his way home from a visit to a distant city. When he stopped to rest for a few days at a friend's home, he spent a night with the friend's daughter. Her name was Aethra. Soon Aegeus departed for Athens, leaving the maiden pregnant.

The child turned out to be a boy, whom Aethra named Theseus. As the years went by, he grew into a handsome, bright, and ambitious young man. He also learned about his real identity. That made him determined to journey to Athens to meet his royal father.

On the way, Theseus encountered dangerous thieves and murderers who had been terrorizing the villages outside Athens' walls. One after the other, he fought and killed these disreputable characters. That earned him a reputation as a hero among the Athenians, and King Aegeus invited him to a lavish banquet.

Theseus' name is linked with the Minotaur, a monster that was half man and half bull.

15

The Young Stranger

At first Aegeus did not realize that the young stranger was actually his son. So the woman the king was then living with, a sorceress named Medea, took advantage of his ignorance. She figured out who Theseus was. Worried that Aegeus would spend more time with him than with her, she convinced the king that the youth was a criminal. He was out to seize the throne, she warned. Believing her, the king allowed her to poison Theseus' wine.

Just when the young man began to drink, however, Aegeus recognized Theseus' sword as one he had given to the maiden Aethra years before. This convinced the king that the young stranger was his son. As the treacherous Medea fled, Aegeus happily welcomed the youth and told the Athenians that Theseus was his son and heir.

Mission to Crete

Not long after the cheerful reunion of father and son, Aegeus told Theseus about the problems the Athenians faced. The biggest was their destructive relationship with Minos, king of the large Greek island of Crete. Minos, who had a larger army than Aegeus did, had threatened to destroy Athens. The only way this could be avoided was for Aegeus to send seven young men and seven young women to Crete each year. When these hostages arrived on the island, Minos threw them into a dungeon with many rooms and corridors. It was called the Labyrinth. Inside dwelled a horrifying monster known as the Minotaur. Half man and half bull, one by one it killed and ate the hostages.

A fresco was restored on the walls of the ruins of the Knossus Palace in Crete. Legend has it that the mazelike palace belonged to King Minos and housed the Minotaur Theseus fought.

A Promise

Hearing about this annual murder of Athenian youths, Theseus was outraged. Determined to stop it, he joined the next group of hostages selected to depart for Crete. He told Aegeus that if he was successful in slaying the Minotaur and freeing the hostages, on his ship's return to Athens it would bear a white sail. If Theseus was unsuccessful, however, his ship would fly a black sail. That would signal that he had been killed.

On reaching Crete, Theseus allowed himself to be thrown into the Labyrinth. According to the ancient Greek writer Apollodorus:

> When he came upon the Minotaur in the farthest corner of the Labyrinth, he killed [it] with his bare hands and then . . . found his way out again. [Later, however, Theseus] forgot as he was sailing back to port to hoist the white sail on his ship.

As the ship approached Athens, Aegeus was watching it from the top of the Acropolis, Athens' rocky central hill. Seeing the black sail, he assumed his son was dead and jumped to his death. Thereafter, the legends say, the waterway between Crete and mainland Greece came to be known as the Aegean Sea in honor of Aegeus.

Theseus slew the Minotaur in his lair. But the hero forgot one vital thing on his return home.

King of Athens

After burying and grieving for his father, Theseus became king of Athens. He went on to unify the central city with the many towns and villages surrounding it. In so doing, he created the Athenian city-state. It became Greece's most influential and accomplished state, and its people never forgot the great hero who had made this possible.

Jason and the Argonauts

During the years when Theseus was a child growing up not far from Athens, another Greek hero was undertaking a great voyage of adventure. He was Jason, a native of the city of Iolcos, in Thessaly. Located in the center of mainland Greece, Thessaly was known for its many thriving farms and horse-breeding stables.

Good Education

The region was also known for a large cave on the slopes of Mount Pelion, where a kindly centaur named Chiron lived. (A centaur was a creature with a humanlike upper half and a horselike lower half.) Chiron regularly took in and educated young men, many of whom later became renowned heroes. One of them was Jason. His name meant healing, perhaps because his native region had many experts in the healing arts. It is likely that Jason, who grew into a handsome young man, learned these arts, along with how to ride horses, from Chiron.

Unlike most centaurs, Chiron was intelligent and cultured.

Jason was an infant when his mother left him in Chiron's care. She did this to keep the child safe. Jason's uncle, the ruthless tyrant Pelias, had recently stolen the throne of Iolcos from Jason's father, Aeson, and she feared the new king would kill the baby.

The Tyrant's Test

When Jason reached young manhood, he decided to leave Mount Pelion and journey to Iolcos. He hoped that Pelias would see reason and give the throne to its rightful owner. Because Aeson was now dead, that owner was Jason. However, Pelias did not want to give up the power and luxury he had come to enjoy. So he devised a way to get rid of Jason, while appearing to be a reasonable man. Lying through his teeth, Pelias claimed that Jason would indeed receive the throne. But first he needed to prove himself worthy of that honor. Jason must find the marvelous and magical fleece of the legendary Golden Ram and bring it back to Iolcos. The fleece lay in the distant land of Colchis, on the shores of the Black Sea. Pelias therefore reasoned that Jason would spend years searching for it, or maybe even die along the way.

Name:
Jason

Roman name:
Jason

Family:
son of Aeson, nephew of tyrant King Pelias of Iolcos

Known for:
quest to find the fleece of the legendary Golden Ram and bring it back to Iolcos on his ship, the *Argo*, with his crew, the Argonauts

The Argonauts

Pelias did not imagine Jason's tremendous courage and resolve. Rising to the challenge, the young man quickly found a suitable ship. It was the *Argo*, named for its builder, the master seaman Argus. Jason also gathered a crew made up of some of Greece's toughest, most accomplished men. Among others, they included the mighty strongman Heracles; the valiant warrior Peleus; the expert musician Orpheus; and the agile and clever Castor and Pollux (who were twin sons of the god Zeus and a mortal woman). In keeping with their ship's name, the crew became known as the Argonauts.

Voyage of the Argo

The Argonauts' journey to Colchis was fraught with danger and strange situations. Among the oddest was the discovery of a group of incredibly smelly women on the Aegean island of Lemnos. These women stank so badly that their husbands had abandoned them. After taking pity on the women and helping them purge their awful odors, Jason and his men continued their journey. Soon they were attacked by a band of ugly, six-armed giants. Fortunately the giants were no match for the powerful Heracles, who defeated and killed them all. In still another weird adventure, the Argonauts drove away a flock of Harpies, repulsive flying creatures with pointed beaks and sharp claws.

Jason was a brave hero. He led his Argonauts to capture the Golden Fleece.

Fire-Breathing Bulls

Several more colorful exploits ensued before Jason and his Argonauts finally arrived in the exotic land of Colchis. Going ashore, Jason sought out and conferred with the Colchian king, Aeetes. Jason said he had come for the fleece. But Aeetes told him that he must first pass a test of courage. Among other things, it consisted of yoking two huge fire-breathing bulls and forcing them to plow the earth. Jason agreed to tackle this test of strength and bravery. Fortunately he had the secret help of Aeetes' daughter, Medea, a sorceress who had fallen in love with Jason shortly after his arrival. She gave him magical ointment that amplified his strength and confidence. According to Apollonius of Rhodes, the ancient Greek writer who told Jason's story:

> From somewhere in the bowels of the earth . . . the pair of bulls appeared, breathing flames of fire. The Argonauts were terrified at the sight. But Jason, planting his feet apart, stood to receive them. [He] held his shield in front of him, and the two bulls, bellowing loudly, charged and butted it with their strong horns [and] snorted and spurted from their mouths devouring flames. . . . The deadly heat assailed him on all sides with the force of lightning. But he was protected by Medea's magic. Seizing the right-hand bull by the tip of its horn, he dragged it with all his might toward the yoke and then brought it down on its knees.

Mission Accomplished

In a similar manner, Jason managed to yoke the second bull. He also defeated a small army of warriors that rapidly grew from seeds planted when the fiery bulls plowed the earth. Yet though Jason had passed the test, Aeetes refused to give him the fleece. Luckily for the

With Medea's help, Jason triumphed to capture the Golden Fleece.

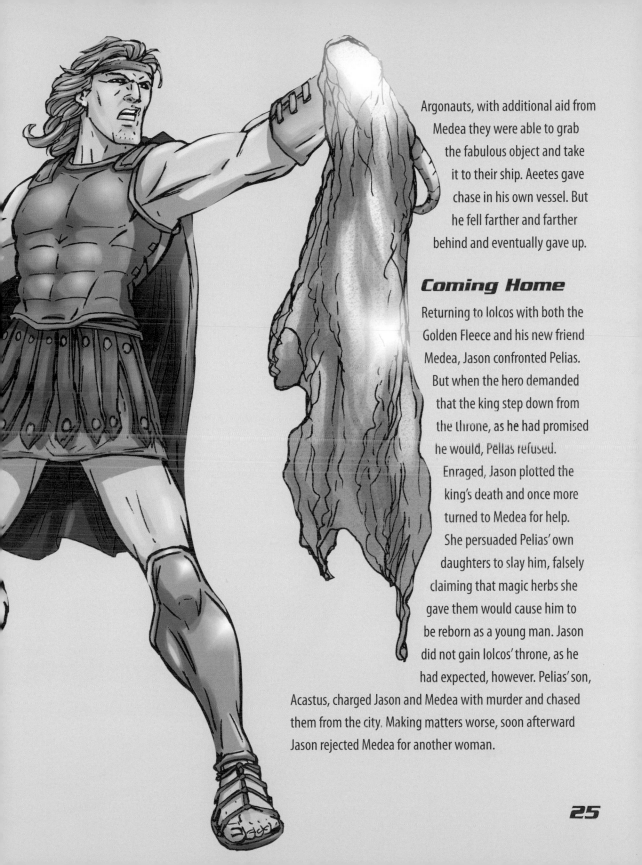

Argonauts, with additional aid from Medea they were able to grab the fabulous object and take it to their ship. Aeetes gave chase in his own vessel. But he fell farther and farther behind and eventually gave up.

Coming Home

Returning to Iolcos with both the Golden Fleece and his new friend Medea, Jason confronted Pelias. But when the hero demanded that the king step down from the throne, as he had promised he would, Pelias refused. Enraged, Jason plotted the king's death and once more turned to Medea for help. She persuaded Pelias' own daughters to slay him, falsely claiming that magic herbs she gave them would cause him to be reborn as a young man. Jason did not gain Iolcos' throne, as he had expected, however. Pelias' son, Acastus, charged Jason and Medea with murder and chased them from the city. Making matters worse, soon afterward Jason rejected Medea for another woman.

Fame to Disgrace

Jason was one of the few Greek heroes who went from achieving admirable deeds to committing scandalous misdeeds. This did not shock or upset the Greeks who told and retold his story. They knew how easy it was for someone of high stature to fall from grace. Many of them saw Jason's descent into disgrace as a cautionary tale from the gods. It warned that all mortals, including the most famous and powerful, are in the end only human, and as such capable of human error and corruption.

Name:
Achilles

Roman name:
Achilles

Family:
son of sea nymph Thetis and Peleus, king of the Myrmidons

Known for:
dying after Paris shot an arrow into his only weak spot, his heel

Achilles was a great Greek warrior who killed Hector during the Trojan War.

Achilles and Odysseus

Among the greatest heroes Greece ever produced, Achilles and Odysseus fought in the 10-year-long Trojan War. Achilles was the most skilled and fearsome warrior in the Greek camp, while Odysseus was the cleverest. Achilles fought against Troy's mightiest champion, Hector. After killing Hector, Achilles tied his enemy's body to his chariot and dragged it around the city. But a Trojan arrow soon ended Achilles' life. Later Odysseus came up with the bright idea of placing Greek soldiers inside a huge wooden horse. This plan allowed the Greeks to win the war. The exciting stories of Achilles and Odysseus were told in detail in the Greek poet Homer's epic tales, the Iliad *and* Odyssey.

Perseus Slays Medusa

The famous Greek hero Perseus spent his childhood on the Aegean island of Seriphos. When he had grown into a young man, the island's king, Polydectes, announced his own future marriage. Polydectes asked for each man in the kingdom to give him a horse as a wedding present. But Perseus owned no horses. So the king told him to bring him back a different gift—the head of the monster Medusa.

Medusa, who lived on a remote island, was a hideous female creature with snakes for hair. Her gaze was so terrifying that anyone who looked directly at her immediately turned to stone. At first Perseus had no idea how to go about killing Medusa. But the goddess Athena gave him a shield made of polished bronze. The young man also had winged sandals that allowed him to fly and a special cap that made him invisible.

Wasting no time, Perseus flew to Medusa's island and found her sleeping on a rock. As he got close to her, she woke up. Since he was invisible, she could smell him, but not see him. She looked in all directions, trying to figure out where he was. Meanwhile, Perseus looked at Medusa only through her reflection in his polished shield, thus avoiding turning to stone. Swooping down, he swung his sword and chopped off her head, which dropped into a sack he was carrying.

Once beautiful, Medusa became a horrifying Gorgon, a monster with snakes for hair.

Chapter 3
MORE MYTHICAL MORTALS

The stories of Greek mythology feature a great many mortals—ordinary humans who tried to do their best to make it through their daily lives. Some of these stories involve love and the search for happiness. Others are about characters burdened with personal flaws such as greed, arrogance, or selfishness. They usually learn a moral lesson the hard way in the end. Still other myths are tragedies, in which people are swept up in events beyond their control and, as a result, suffer extreme hardship or even death.

The Tragedy of Oedipus

Of those tragedies, perhaps none is sadder or more heartrending than the tale of Oedipus. A tall, handsome, well-built man, he was a prince of the city of Corinth, which is several miles west of Athens in southern Greece. In addition to being blessed with good looks, the young man was intelligent, well-educated, and just and ethical in his dealings with others. All of these admirable attributes gave him the ability to deal quickly and fairly with emergencies and other problems. They also equipped him with the tools needed to become an effective leader, including the ruler of a kingdom.

Fear of the Oracle

Partly because he was so upstanding and well-meaning, Oedipus was extremely disturbed at what he heard while visiting an oracle. (An oracle was a person thought to have the ability to convey messages from the gods to humans. The place where he or she delivered these messages was also called an oracle.) The oracle told him that some day he would kill his father and marry his mother. Because Oedipus believed the prediction had come from a god, he worried that it was accurate. So he decided to get as far away from his parents—the king and queen of Corinth—as he could. That way, he reasoned, there would be no way that the prophecy could ever come true.

Oedipus was desperate to avoid the fate that had been predicted by the oracle.

Oedipus and the Sphinx

For this reason, Oedipus bade his family farewell and moved to Thebes, which lay many miles to the northeast. No sooner had he reached the large, prosperous city when he learned that it was being terrorized by a frightening monster. Called the Sphinx, it had the body of a winged lion and the face of a human woman. It was also large and strong enough to tear people apart and devour them alive. Hearing that many Thebans had been slain by the creature, Oedipus took it upon himself to stop the slaughter. He confronted the Sphinx and cleverly maneuvered it into plunging off a towering cliff to its death.

French artist Ingres painted the encounter between Oedipus and the strange beast known as the Sphinx.

The overjoyed citizens of Thebes were so thankful to the brave stranger that they made him their king. Not long afterward, Oedipus married Jocasta, the widow of the city's former king, Laius, who had been killed on a roadside while on a journey to another city. Oedipus and Jocasta had four children together and enjoyed several years of happiness.

Plague as a Punishment

A terrible plague struck Thebes, however, and hundreds of people died. Jocasta's brother, Creon, consulted an oracle, who gave him disturbing news. The plague, the oracle said, was a punishment for the murder of Jocasta's first husband, King Laius. Only when the killer was brought to justice would the epidemic end.

The stalwart Oedipus vowed to find the murderer and thereby save the city. But before the king could gather his soldiers and begin the search, a blind Theban named Teiresias approached him. Teiresias, who possessed the god-given gift of prophecy, told Oedipus something shocking. He said Oedipus was the man who had slain Laius.

"You are the unholy defilement [corruption] of this land," Teiresias shouted.

> You are a pitiful figure. [You] who have eyes, cannot see the evil in which you stand. . . . Do you even know who your parents are? Without knowing it, you are the enemy of your own flesh and blood, the dead below and the living here above. The double edged curse of your mother and father [will] one day drive you from this land. You see straight now but then you will see darkness. You will scream aloud on that day, [for] there is no man alive whose ruin will be more pitiful than yours.

Name:
Oedipus

Roman name:
Oedipus

Family:
married to Jocasta, who turned out to be his mother; father was King Laius

Known for:
mistakenly killing his father and marrying his mother

A messenger arrived with terrible news for the Theban king Oedipus and his wife Jocasta.

Stranger at a Crossroads

At first Oedipus thought that Teiresias was badly mistaken. But then the king's wife, Jocasta, told Oedipus what had happened on the day Laius was killed. An unknown person had murdered the former king at a crossroads, she explained. Hearing this, Oedipus froze. He suddenly remembered that years before, when he was on his way to Thebes, he had killed a man he did not know at a crossroads. Had that man been King Laius, he wondered?

Terrible Secret

At that tense moment, a messenger arrived from Corinth to announce that the king of that city had recently died. Oedipus was saddened by this news. Even worse for him, however, the messenger now proceeded to reveal a terrible secret. Oedipus was not the son of Corinth's royal rulers, he said. In reality, he was the child of the king and queen of Thebes. A few days after his birth, they had decided they did not want him and had left him outside to die. Fortunately, a servant had taken pity on and saved the infant, who had ended up being raised by the Corinthian king and queen.

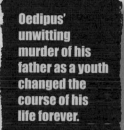

Victim of Cruel Fate

Oedipus now grasped the horrible truth—that he was an unwitting victim of fate and the will of the gods. The man he had killed at the crossroads had been his father, and his present wife, Jocasta, was his mother. The oracle's dreadful prophecy had come true! Overcome with guilt and disgust, Jocasta hanged herself, while Oedipus screamed aloud, seized a brooch pin, and gashed out his eyes. Now blind and pitiful, just as Teiresias had predicted he would be, he wandered aimlessly away. That left Creon to rule the horrified and grief-stricken Theban people. Because Oedipus married his mother, today a grown man with an unusually close relationship with his mother is sometimes said to have an "Oedipus complex."

Pandora, the First Woman

Fate, oracles, and prophecies aside, the anguish and pain Oedipus and Jocasta experienced may not have been their fault. Indeed these ills, along with those suffered by all Greeks, may have been the result of a mistake made many centuries before they were born. One of the most famous Greek myths claims that when humans first appeared, troubles such as hatred, greed, fear, lust, pain, and so forth did not yet exist. Moreover, these ills came to plague humanity because of a poor decision made by the first woman. Her name was Pandora.

Pandora was absolutely gorgeous. She was also wonderfully talented in many ways. She came to acquire these positive traits because several of the Olympian gods contributed to shaping her. Hephaestus, god of the forge and an exceedingly skilled craftsman, molded her body from a piece of clay. He was inspired by the lovely features of two or three of the most attractive goddesses.

Next Athena, goddess of wisdom, created a wardrobe made up of strikingly beautiful outfits for the young woman. The goddess also instructed her in the arts of spinning and weaving. After that, the goddess of beauty, Aphrodite, taught the girl how to walk and move with grace and dignity. Another divine teacher, Hermes, patron god of literature, showed her how to speak in a pleasant, appealing voice. Considering the young woman's impressive collection of talents and abilities, it is no wonder that her divine mentors gave her the name Pandora, which means "all gifts."

The beautiful Pandora is said to be responsible for the world's miseries.

Before Pandora

In a way Pandora's story began even before she received these gifts. The mighty Zeus, leader of the Olympian gods, decided to populate the Earth with a race of beings. They should look like the gods, he said. But they should lack the immortality and great powers possessed by the gods. For the task of creating the human race, Zeus selected Prometheus, a member of an earlier group of gods, the Titans.

Creatures of Prometheus

Prometheus began by collecting special mud that contained tiny sparks of life. These sparks had originated long before, during the creation of the world and sky by the earliest divine forces. The humans made from this mud appropriately received the nickname "creatures of Prometheus." At first all of the humans were male. Zeus decided that there must be a female gender as well. So he ordered Hephaestus to create a woman and allowed several other gods to endow her with various abilities.

The Sealed Jar

Next Zeus told Hermes to guide Pandora to Earth, along with a large, sealed jar. The young woman had no idea what was in the jar. Also following Zeus' orders, Hermes introduced Pandora to the Titan Epimetheus, who was Prometheus' brother. Epimetheus was captivated by the girl's beauty and welcomed her into his home as his wife.

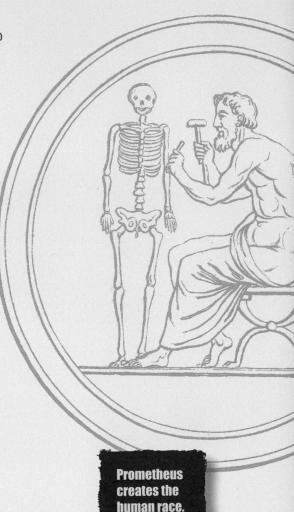

Prometheus creates the human race.

When Prometheus heard about these events, he became concerned. He knew that his brother was kind and well-meaning. But Epimetheus was also a bit dim-witted, and Prometheus worried that the wily Zeus was trying to trick him somehow. In fact, Prometheus had more than once warned Epimetheus never to accept any gifts from Zeus.

This suspicion of the chief Olympian's motives proved to be well-founded. Pandora became more and more curious about the contents of the jar Zeus had given her. Finally she could no longer contain her curiosity. With Epimetheus' aid, she opened the container and immediately a flood of troubles and evils spewed out and spread across the world. These ills have afflicted humanity ever since. Zeus had reasoned that, with so many problems of their own to deal with, humans would never have the time or energy to rebel against the gods.

Greedy Midas

One of the evils that Pandora accidentally unleashed was greed, which later infected many mortals. One of them was an ancient nobleman named Midas. He had inherited the throne of Phrygia, in central Asia Minor (what is now Turkey) from his father, King Gordius. No physical descriptions of Midas have survived. But it was said that he loved giving long, lavish parties in which huge amounts of food and drink were consumed. So it is likely that he was at least a bit roly-poly, if not downright fat. His gluttony also extended to other objects. These included fine clothes, expensive furniture, and gold rings and other costly jewelry.

In fact, Midas was so obsessed with owning gold that it eventually got him into a serious predicament. One day he encountered the famous satyr Silenus. (A satyr was a creature that was half man and half goat.) What made Silenus so well-known was that he was both tutor and friend to the god of fertility and wine, Dionysus. Hoping to impress the god, Midas invited Silenus to a party. It lasted 10 days and the satyr thoroughly enjoyed himself. Then Midas personally escorted Silenus over the mountains to a temple that Dionysus was visiting.

Glutton for Gold

Dionysus was so thankful to Midas for entertaining his friend that he granted the mortal king anything he wished for. It did not take the greedy Midas long to decide what he wanted.

Name:
Midas

Roman name:
Midas

Family:
adopted by King Gordius and goddess Cybele

Known for:
his so-called Midas touch; his obsession with gold led to his being granted his wish of turning anything he touched into gold

Midas ended up hating the gift that he had so coveted. His golden touch was a curse, and in later versions of the myth, he turned his own daughter to gold.

40

He asked for the ability to turn anything he touched into gold. Dionysus smiled and agreed to the request. Then Midas headed for home, thinking about nothing but the enormous amounts of gold he would soon have.

It soon became clear, however, that Midas had made a serious mistake. True, he was thrilled when he touched rocks, sticks, chairs, and clay pots and they instantly turned to gold. But then he grew hungry and sat down to eat his supper.

To his surprise and horror, his meat, fruit, and other foods transformed into gold the second he picked them up. By the end of the second day, he was starving.

Change of Heart

The desperate Midas prayed to Dionysus and begged
him to take back the gift he had given. The god appeared
and smiled once more, for he had known all along what
would happen to Midas. In a benevolent gesture, he told
the king that he would return to normal if he washed
himself in the Pactolus River. Midas did as Dionysus
instructed and was delighted to find himself cured. Some
legends claim that the bath Midas took that day gave rise
to the unusual amount of gold dust found in the Pactolus
riverbed in later ages. In later centuries a person who
enjoyed unusually good luck in accumulating money or
valuables was said to have the "Midas touch."

**King Midas
followed the
advice of
Dionysus and
bathed in the
Pactolus River.**

Vain Narcissus

Another common human frailty that escaped from Pandora's jar was vanity. Only a few people were tainted by extreme self-love over the years. But those so afflicted usually made others unhappy, and in time they themselves suffered from unhappiness or even worse misfortunes.

One of the saddest cases was that of Narcissus. He was born in a bygone age, the son of a river god named Cephissus and a nymph named Liriope. It might have been because the father and mother were both extremely good-looking that their child was also quite attractive. In fact Narcissus grew into one of the most stunningly handsome mortals in the known world. Unfortunately for him, and others as well, he became incredibly conceited. That made dealing with him a miserable and sometimes even dangerous experience.

Love at First Sight

The misery Narcissus caused was illustrated by the fact tht many young women fell in love with him almost at first sight. Some tried to strike up friendships with him. Others proposed marriage to him. Still others offered him valuable gifts if he would spend just a few hours with them. But all these earnest efforts were in vain. Thinking he was too handsome, and too good, for any of them, he rejected them one by one.

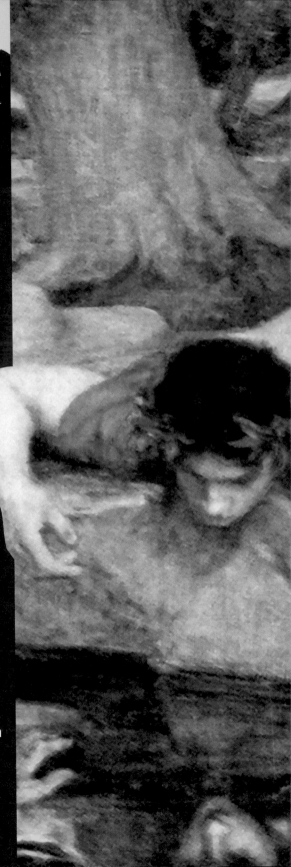

Sad Echo

The heartbreaking case of the nymph Echo shows the danger that Narcissus could pose to someone who was innocent and vulnerable. Both beautiful and kind, Echo fell in love with Narcissus just as many other nymphs and human women had. She tried to get to know him. However, he coldly walked right by her. No matter how hard she tried to get his attention, he callously ignored her, as if she did not exist. Echo was so badly wounded by this cruel treatment that she lost more and more weight. Gradually she wasted away until all that was left of her was her voice. This is the origin of the term "echo," which means a sound that grows increasingly feeble until it dissipates into nothingness.

Beautiful Reflection

The goddess of beauty, Aphrodite, soon heard about Echo's sad fate and was disgusted by Narcissus' mean-spirited behavior. She decided to teach the youth a lesson. Moreover, she cleverly used his own vanity against him. Noticing that he was sitting at the edge of a pond, she caused him to look at his own reflection in the water. Then, with a wave of her hand, she made him fall in love with that image. Day after day, he kept staring at his handsome visage. Weeks went by. The weeks turned into months, and still Narcissus could not take his eyes off of himself. Eventually, just as Echo had, he wasted away and died. As a result, he was never again able to break a woman's heart. His name did not perish, however. In later times, people who seemed a bit too in love with themselves came to be called narcissists.

Narcissus was a beautfful young man. But he was cursed with vanity and loved only himself.

The mulberry tree was the meeting place for tragic young lovers Pyramis and Thisbe.

46

Pyramis and Thisbe

Although Narcissus loved only himself, the Greeks had several myths about traditional love between men and women. One of the most beautiful is the story of the teenage lovers Pyramis and Thisbe, who lived in the great city of Babylon, lying many miles east of Greece. The pair lived next door to each other and became close friends. Eventually Pyramis and Thisbe fell in love and told their parents they wanted to become husband and wife. But the parents thought they were too young and did their best to keep the two from seeing each other.

Pyramis and Thisbe decided to run away together and agreed on a secret plan. They would sneak out of their houses in the middle of the night. Then they would meet at a mulberry tree covered with white berries. Thisbe made it to the tree first. While she was waiting for her lover to arrive, she was horrified to see a lion moving toward her. Terrified that she might be killed,

she ran away, but as she did so she accidentally dropped the scarf she was wearing. The lion, with a bloody mouth from a recent meal, found the scarf and ripped it with its teeth. But it soon lost interest and walked away into the night.

A few minutes later, Pyramis reached the tree. Finding the blood-covered scarf, he believed that Thisbe was dead. Overcome with grief, he pulled out his knife and stabbed himself in the heart. A minute later, Thisbe returned to the tree. When she saw the lifeless body of Pyramis, she burst into tears. Then she pulled the knife from his chest and plunged it into her own.

On finding out about the tragedy, the gods were saddened. They noticed that the blood of Pyramis had spurted onto the tree's white berries. So in memory of the young lovers, the gods decided that from then on the mulberry tree would produce only deep red fruit.

Europa's Unexpected Voyage

Zeus, leader of the Olympian gods, not only caused the first mortal woman to be made but also had affairs with many mortal women behind the back of his divine wife, Hera. One of the most famous of these affairs was with Europa. She was the daughter of the king of Tyre, a port town on the Mediterranean Sea's eastern coast.

One day Zeus caught sight of the beautiful young Europa strolling on a beach near her home. He was immediately attracted to her and devised an unusual plan to win her over. He disguised himself as a bull and got her to sit for a while on his back. But before she could climb down again, he jumped into the sea and started swimming, making waves and spraying her with a refreshing mist. To Europa's surprise, the unexpected voyage took them all the way to Crete.

There Europa and Zeus had three sons. One of them, Minos, became king of Crete. Later still, the continent in which Greece rests was named Europe after Europa. Also, Zeus celebrated his affair with her by placing a bull's image in the sky. It became known as the constellation of Taurus, part of the famous Zodiac.

The planet Jupiter is named for the Roman version of Zeus' name. Of that giant planet's four largest moons, one is called Europa, after the mythical Greek maiden.

The Fierce Amazons

To the classical Greeks, the troubles associated with Pandora sometimes seemed endless. For instance, some of the storytellers of those times felt that her creation and that of other early women was in a way a curse on Greek men. This was partly because they believed wives began to nag and make demands on their husbands. It was also because the Greeks of the Age of Heroes were beset by a series of wars with a group of aggressive women. They were known as the Amazons. According to legend the Amazons' nation was populated only by women. The location of that nation varied from story to story. But the most common belief was that it rested somewhere in the vast steppes situated north of the Black Sea (in what is now southern Russia).

According to most ancient writers, the name Amazon derived from a strange custom these women practiced. Supposedly each of them sliced off one of her breasts to make it easier for her to wield a bow and spear. Even if this grisly practice was nothing but hearsay, the fact is that the Greek word a-mazos meant "without breast."

Name:
Amazons

Roman name:
Amazons

Family:
all-female group of powerful warriors from the steppes north of the Black Sea

Known for:
their exceptional hunting and fighting prowess

Amazons were fearless fighters during the Greek Age of Heroes.

Hunting and Fighting

Using weapons was important to the Amazons because they had a very warlike society. They claimed that they were directly descended from Ares, the Greek god of war, whom they worshipped. Because they spent much of their time hunting, they also prayed to Artemis, the goddess who oversaw wild animals and hunting. To become effective warriors and hunters, the women exercised vigorously and trained hard with various weapons from an early age. They also raised horses and became expert riders. Myths about the Amazons claim that each of them was at least a match for the average male Greek soldier.

Battles between Greek men and the Amazons gave rise to a word in the Greek language for this sort of fighting—Amazonomachy. Many Greek heroes were said to have fought the warrior women. One was the mighty strongman Heracles, while performing one of his 12 Labors. His goal was to steal the wide belt belonging to the Amazonian queen, Hippolyta. He had to fight her and several of her followers to get it. Another clash between Amazons and Greeks occurred during the famous Trojan War. Another Amazonian queen, Penthesilea, sided with the Trojans in the conflict. So the finest warrior among the Greeks who besieged Troy, Achilles, attacked and slew her. In a weird and disturbing turn of events, he claimed he fell in love with her after she was dead.

Fearsome Amazon warriors could even bring down a lion.

Hippolyta and Theseus

Perhaps the biggest and bloodiest of all the Greek-Amazonian wars was the one involving Hippolyta and the great Athenian hero Theseus. The conflict began not long after he had brought together all the Athenian villages and towns into a united nation-state. For reasons that are now somewhat unclear, Theseus decided to journey to Amazonian territory. He gathered a force of well-armed Athenian soldiers and sailed northward to the coast of Asia Minor. Eventually the party reached the homeland of the Amazons and went ashore.

Ancient sources differ on what happened next. But several say that Hippolyta sent her younger sister, Antiope, to greet the strangers. Antiope brought gifts for the Greek leader. She also tried to establish diplomatic relations between the two peoples. However, for reasons that are uncertain Theseus suddenly took her prisoner and sailed back to Athens. Another ancient source claims that Theseus and his men attempted to establish a Greek town in Amazonian territory.

Angry Amazons

Whatever the Greeks did on that fateful expedition, it greatly angered Hippolyta and the other Amazons. The warrior women wasted no time in gathering their weapons and preparing for war. When they were ready, they headed southeastward toward Greece. After a long and difficult trek, they finally reached Athenian territory in September and marched on Athens' central town.

On hearing that the Amazons were approaching, Theseus hastily mustered the Athenian men. They donned their armor as quickly as they could. Then, following the king's orders, some climbed the Acropolis to guard the palace and temples that rested atop that rocky hill. The soldiers also helped the Athenian women and children take refuge there. The rest of the armed men formed ranks in a long line that snaked across one side of the town. The Amazons also formed a line. Facing the Greeks head on, it stretched across the other side of the town.

When the Athenian hero Theseus fought the Amazons, it became an almighty battle.

Let the Battle Begin

A tense pause ensued. Both sides stood their ground in utter silence for an unknown number of minutes. Then Theseus gave the order to attack. The ancient Greek writer Plutarch described the battle:

> The Athenians engaged the [Amazons'] left wing. [On] this flank, the women routed the Athenians and forced them back as far as the shrine of the Eumenides [mythical friendly spirits]. But on the other side, the Athenians who attacked the Amazons . . . drove their right wing back to their camp and killed great numbers of them.

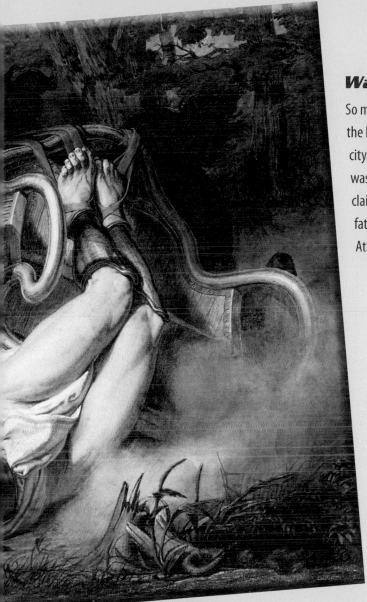

War and Peace

So many Amazons were slain that day that they lost the battle and retreated to a point well outside the city. Some versions of the myth say that Hippolyta was killed by a javelin during the fighting. Others claim she survived the battle. Whatever her fate may have been, Plutarch suggests that the Athenians and Amazons decided to make peace:

> We have at least some evidence that the war was ended by a treaty. The proof of this is the name of the place adjoining the Theseum [a temple honoring the god Hephaestus] which is called Horcomosium ["place where oaths are sworn"], because of the oaths [each side gave the other] there, and also the sacrifice which in [ages past] was offered to the Amazons before the festival of Theseus.

Exactly what happened to the Amazons in the centuries that followed the war is unknown. What is certain, however, is that their name survives. In modern times people sometimes call a large, strong woman an Amazon. This is only one of thousands of words and names from the ancient Greek myths that have become part of modern life.

Queen Hippolyta may have died in battle, but the name of the Amazons was to live on.

HERACLES' 12 LABORS

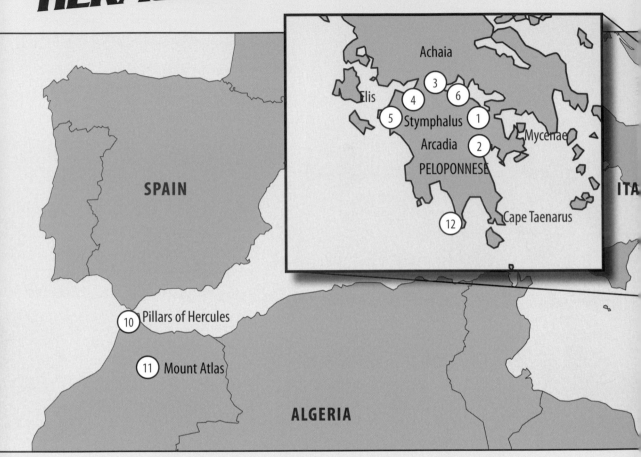

Labor		Location
1	Hide of Nemean Lion	Nemea (Argolid)
2	Lerna Hydra	Lerna (Argolid)
3	Cerynitian Hind	Ceryneia (Achaia)
4	Erymanthian Boar	Mount Erymanthos (Arcadia)
5	Augeian Stables	Elis (West Peloponnese)
6	Stymphalian Birds	Lake Stymphalus (Arcadia)

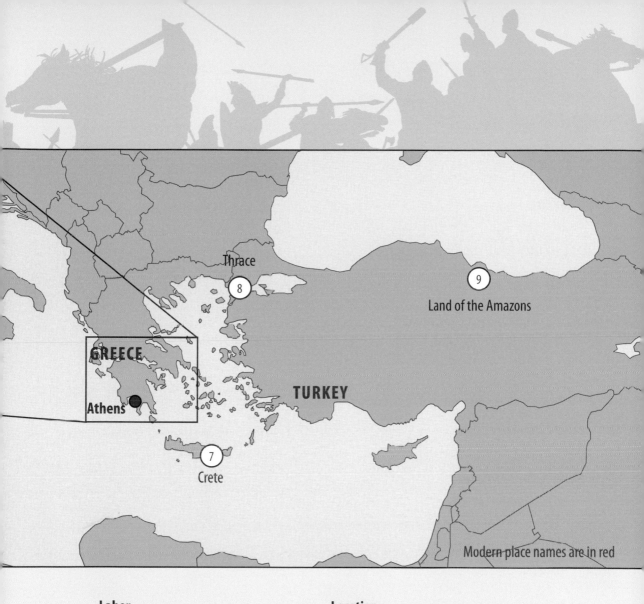

Thrace

⑧

⑨

Land of the Amazons

GREECE

TURKEY

Athens •

⑦

Crete

Modern place names are in red

Labor		Location
⑦	Cretan Bull	Crete
⑧	Diomedes' Mares	Thrace
⑨	Belt of Amazon Hippolyta	North Asia Minor
⑩	The Cattle of Geryon	Near Straits of Gibraltar
⑪	Apples of Hesperides	Somewhere in Libya
⑫	Capture of Cerberus	Hades, near Cape Taenarus in Peloponnese

ADDITIONAL RESOURCES

Further Reading

Daly, Kathleen N. *Greek and Roman Mythology A to Z.*
New York: Chelsea House, 2009.

Green, Roger L. *Tales of the Greek Heroes.*
London: Puffin, 2009.

Hamby, Zachary. *Mythology for Teens: Classic Myths for Today's World.*
Austin, Texas: Prufrock Press, 2009.

Kurth, Steve. *Hercules: The Twelve Labors.*
Minneapolis: Graphic Universe, 2007.

Smith, Charles R. *The Mighty 12: Superheroes of the Greek Myths.*
New York: Little, Brown, 2008.

Internet Sites

Use FactHound to find Internet sites related to this book. All of the sites on FactHound have been researched by our staff.

Here's all you do:
Visit *www.facthound.com*
Type in this code:
9780756544805

GLOSSARY

Age of Heroes the period of the distant past in which the classical Greeks believed the stories told in their myths took place. Modern scholars call that era Greece's late Bronze Age and date it from about 1500 BC to 1150 BC.

Amazonomachy in Greek mythology, fierce battles between men and Amazons

Amazons in Greek mythology, a race of warrior women

Argonauts the crew of the *Argo*, the ancient Greek hero Jason's ship

boar a wild pig

centaur a mythical creature that was half man and half horse

city-state in ancient Greece, a small nation consisting of a central town and outlying villages and farms

classical Greeks modern scholars date Greece's Classical Age to about 500 BC to 323 BC. More generally, the inhabitants of Greece between about 800 BC and 300 BC.

constellation group of stars seen from Earth. Many were named by the ancient Greeks for animals or mythological people

divine godlike

epic a long poem, usually describing heroic acts

fleece the woolen coat or skin of a sheep or goat

forge a smithy, or a place where metals are worked, by heating and hammering

gluttony greed for food or objects

Harpies mythical flying creatures with sharp claws and beaks

immortality a state of living forever

labyrinth a maze; in Greek mythology the Labyrinth was a mass of rooms on Crete that housed the fearsome Minotaur.

medieval to do with the Middle Ages, generally from AD mid-400s to the mid 1400s

Minotaur a mythical creature that was half man and half bull

mortal a human being

narcissist unusually vain or self-obsessed person

Olympians the group of gods led by Zeus and thought to live on top of Mount Olympus, Greece's highest mountain

oracle in the ancient world, a person, usually a priestess, thought to be a medium between the gods and humans; or the building in which an oracle passed on a message from the gods; or the message itself

prophecy the art or process of foretelling the future; or a specific prediction

prophet a person thought to be able to predict events

ruthless hardhearted, showing no kindness

satyr a mythical creature that was half man and half goat

Sphinx a mythical monster having the body of a lion, wings, and a woman's face

steppe a grassy plain

supernatural extraordinary, otherworldly

Titans race of gods that ruled the universe before the rise of the Olympians

tyrant a leader who rules unfairly, a dictator

SOURCE NOTES

Chapter 1
Truly Timeless Tales
Page 6, line 15: Michael Grant. *Myths of the Greeks and Romans*. New York: Plume, 1995, pp. 45–46.
Page 7, line 6: Ibid., p. 46.

Chapter 2
Three Famous Heroes
Page 18, line 13: Apollodorus of Athens. *Epitome*. Excerpted in Rhoda A. Hendricks, *Classical Gods and Heroes: Myths as Told by the Ancient Authors*. New York: Morrow Quill, 1974, pp. 171–172.
Page 24, line 13: Apollonius of Rhodes. *Argonautica*. Published as *The Voyage of the Argo*. Trans. E.V. Rieu. New York: Penguin, 1971, pp. 143–144.

Chapter 3
More Mythical Mortals
Page 33, line 18: Sophocles. *Oedipus the King*. Trans. Bernard M.W. Knox. New York: Simon and Schuster, 2005, pp. 23, 25, 28.
Page 56, line 9: Plutarch. *Parallel Lives*. Excerpted in *The Rise and Fall of Athens: Nine Greek Lives by Plutarch*. Trans. Ian Scott-Kilvert. New York: Penguin, 1984, p. 33.
Page 57, line 8: Ibid, p. 34.